Hear Our Voice

Tanayah Mcdonald

BookLeaf Publishing

India | USA | UK

Presentation by *BookLeaf Publishing*

Web: www.bookleafpub.com

E-mail: info@bookleafpub.com

ISBN: 9789367397794

First edition 2024

Dedicated to my parents, who could see life through my eyes.

ACKNOWLEDGEMENT

Thank you so much for taking the time to read this book. It is one of the first opportunities my parents have supported me endlessly and I could find great solace if I put myself out there. I want to thank my friends who have motivated me to go beyond and push me to my greatest potential. While I was uncertain, the least I could do was try with maximum effort. Again, thank you for taking the time to read this.

PREFACE

When writing this as a senior, I would never expect the struggles and opportunities given to me throughout high school. Balancing rigorous coursework with a part-time job while preparing for the transition into adulthood has been a mysterious ride of emotions. The occasional crushes and even the issue of having fake friends have shown me many lessons teenagers experience. Now, in my senior year, I feel there is nothing more than focusing on enjoying every last second and balancing my life. As my classmates and I prepare to go our separate ways, my dreams will always remain close to my heart.

In writing these stories, I aim to show teenagers that they are not alone in this transformative process. It's normal to have big dreams and aspirations, but the challenges of life can make one question if they will ever make it. This collection was created to provide solace and inspiration to those who may be facing similar uncertainties on their path to adulthood. I want others to gain the same inspiration to reach your greatest potential and how far you can go. No

matter what, you are not alone and will forever
have the strength to make it through.

What we want the world to know

How about this,
Let me be?

You will see the dream

 so many teens, so many dreams
that we want to achieve
if we just believe
that if we can reach the stars,
then we can go afar
within the dream we made
that is just for us
for us to defend,
  for us to protect,
    for us to grow on,
      and show that although
we made it,

           it

was not easy to make it

whether trying to be the best in what you do
or just trying to be the one that makes it through,
you have to be your best
so you don't fall behind the rest
     you have to be the best
because there is no time to stress
cause no one is going to be the best like you and
me
So how is someone going to tell you who you
need to be?

to be powerful,
to be fearsome,
to be someone with a dream
seems like no one can stop ya
But the only ones who can stop you
is the one who can drop you
whether it can be an ex or a jinx
   that can be gone in a blink
so many things can just happen in one little
blink,
that text you that was delivered can be left
unread
or the many many things that could've been left
unsaid
but why live in the dread
when you get out of bed and get ahead
ahead of the shame,
ahead of the game,
      so you can claim that frame that marks
your name
                              or just you
don't wanna be the one that lives in the same
shame

that will be left in your frame
because no one wants to be in a life of shame
so you can aim for greatness,
as the greatest of all had gone so far

i made this far so i can tell my story,
                    so I can represent my
story,
                            and no one's
going to tell me how to write the story
because I am the only one holding this pencil
and paper
because I deserve to be here, there, and
everywhere
and just before I go,
            no one is like you and me,
                    so keep dreaming because
one day
                                        you
will see the dream finally achieved

broken bonds, fractured visions

We heard the famous Martin speech "I Had A
Dream"
to have what others have without a restriction to
our dreams
Our ancestors fought with blood, sweat, and
tears
To make it happen for everyone if we worked as
a team
But it is not as easy as counting one, two, three
because no one is going to count all the people
we lost before we were
Free

The people ripped limb from limb
Or even shot to death, taking their last breath
While the sisters and brothers prayed
for their health
But no one knows that death comes from all
regardless of whether your skin is darker or
lighter
They still died as fighters fighting for me,
fighting for you,
Fighting for us, fighting for the future

You are probably wondering how this young
woman talks with so much knowledge
I know so much but never went to college,
nothing symbolic
They never said in the rule book that I could
never learn this topic
As there is nothing microscopic about this logic
and how ironic this played for generations
with such high expectations and many
limitations
You don't believe me? Let me give you an
evaluation.

My name is Imani, the original copy
When I was born, nobody told me
in this world that what occurred before me
is repeating in front of me
Including the assumption that my people are
behind
Plaguing my young mind with an inevitable
demise

Growing up with only two pigtails in my hair, a
crooked smile, and only a little doll as her
sidekick
I grew up knowing that if I can achieve anything
Then who was going to tell me how to do
anything?

So, when a boy got mad at me and yanked my
hair,
I scratched him back with these nails

They called my mom working her third shift
Her arms folded, her legs crossed
"How was she wrong to use self-defense?"
"Well, I don't think she will fit with us here."
Us? What's wrong with staying with them?

Is it because my hair is too coily? Too curly?
Was it the fact that my eyes were too big for this
world?
I looked at my mom and kept asking her why
She took my hand and took me away
Mumbled under her breath, "They should never
treat us this way."
"Momma, what do you mean?"

She did not want to tell me that we were
considered a threat
that living in these shackles was a lead
and there was no chance if we even held our
heads
High
So she promised to do big things, already in her
head
That my work will never be slept on

Over time, she kept stressing and stressing
Blessing and blessing that her kid would bring
her success
Progress was being made, and there was no time
for requests
Unless it gave less and less pressure
To be seen as the aggressor

I was always seen as the successor, never the
lesser
If they always thought less, they had to do better
I am not a forgetter, so when I watched history
repeated
With George Floyd, our communities are being
ripped apart
I knew we needed a restart because I knew I was
raised
For this part with all the smarts given
By God's grace

I was born with a voice, there was never a
choice
Either stand for my people or let evil deceive
them
I marched and marched until I was overwhelmed
One fist held high and the other with my poster
Screaming louder over my shoulder as
The holder of our truth and
 The defender of our youth

They threw tear gas to take down my ass
thinking it's gonna leave me to scram like I
gave a damn?
So you know what I did? I stepped into the car
and let all the eyes
Follow me so I can tell them the truth, there is
no room for such lies
I told my people that to make an impact, we
need to create an impact
So many countless acts, nothing behind them but
evident facts
that we attract, we react, we are in fact
The people with dreams, trying to strengthen the
bonds of America

It is all on me, on us to capture that dream
It may seem extreme, but no one else can
redeem
Anything to be seen, to be heard, and more
important
To fix those shattered dreams to make it into
something supreme
Except you and the voice you can use to be seen

A broken pencil, a broken will

One day I saw myself walking in for the first
time
and no one shall tell me I do not belong,
For I am ready to live and experience
more things beyond my will

It will be hard to say goodbye,
To grasp it once more and never again--
I have grown so close to her
that she is now a part of me

Her callused hands have worked and never
stopped
Her eyes strain from the dishes
noticing the children laugh even within their
conditions
She wants to be with them, laugh with them

She tells herself she mustn't dream too much
for it shall hurt her and leave her
husband astray.
She was once a child before, but

Life aged her too soon.

She shall not fight, scream, yell, or cry
but mature and grow
as that is the right thing to do. '

To do, to live, to stay here
Alas, it sounds resemble close to heaven
but as I tell my friend this...
she seems only more concerned.

She wants to hear me,
to see me, to believe me,
but it is so hard to give myself grace
because in this case

I wish I could have said
"I do not want to grow up"
but it would hurt my family's dear heart
as we struggle to keep ourselves up to part
With only little money to keep us with what we
got

I wish I could have said
"I want to hold a pencil"
instead of it breaking in front of my face
because I stepped into the wrong place
I want to be able to learn about girls who look
like me
See how even through adversities and different
diversities,

there will be able to go to prestigious
universities
Even under uncertainty, they knew they were
certain
they could get degrees, a guarantee
to get three figures and feel free

Free of anything that comes along the way,
As ease comes to take away any disease
as it pleases. If I could go to school,
find myself learning the right tools,
I can use it to make the right moves
and improve our financial stability

It is a liability in this big world
to know what you know,
so you can grow and show
others in the future
If they were able to get through
I shall see myself aligning my views

No! I must try. I rather stay by
and help my parents cross the bay
but I cannot deny, deny, deny
For these lies, lies, lies
of not wanting to get an education
and the information to go farther
and harder, so I can get smarter

My knowledge shall become my armor,
My mind shall make me sharper,
The negative thoughts shall get ready to depart,
as I want to be like the children, not separated in
part
 but together to create a new start

I wanted to tell her all these things
but I was told to stay happy, to stay classy
To stay grateful and truthful because silence was
the best answer,
 the best manner

I knew I could help myself
for she helped me,
she believed in me,
She knew that she was more than a broken will
and wanted to reach as far as she could go.

So, I took a deep breath and asked her
"Can I ever dream of learning again?"
with dreams, with aspirations
She took my hand and told me

There is always the possibility.

She decides to take me to a sanctuary
Let me say the last words before we lay her
down to rest

I say that I will forever miss my young self
and let them do the rest

Now, I still think about her
I look at the mirror and think I am losing parts of
my younger self
but she will forever be a part of me
and be the only person to believe in me
so it is time for the best of me and her--
to say our final goodbye.

Dear high school, farewell

I know you will miss me, but I will not miss
you.
When I woke up to find out I had to see you
another day, I wish I could stay
In my bed without having to realize I have six
essays due in one day.
If someone asked me if I would rather stay home
or go to school, I have six words:
Please do not play with me.
I have been here for four years and have only
one question
Why have they not paid me yet?
I think they forgot that I did all these
assignments and ALL these requirements.
In nine months, all that will be on my mind is
walking the stage
Ready to turn the next page, ready for a new
change
But there is so much to do, they think I am going
through
Without being ready to withdraw and say I am
through
All this stuff due, I am so blown
When is my cue to get this cap and gown?
At this point, they just clowning me year-round

Like they have been doing for the past few years
I do not want to drown in any more work
Rather work on my senior pictures, my prom asI
pictured
Maybe do a little things here and there
Just to be fair, I rather do that than be
Here.
I am aware that the end is near
That this year will be our year
And that in thirty-four weeks it will be all soon
They keep repeating this over and over
But I will have to admit
I rather have thirty than have one sixty
Then fifty, then forty,
Then thirty, then twenty,
And then ten.
I am about to tell you the last ten things that I
will ever do
 I will walk these hallways and finally be free
I already foresee my future
I am going to see all these teachers and ask them
where is my fee
I will plan my last senior prank before I flee
I will never have to plea because I will be
smiling in glee
I am too tired to write the last five,
I just want my degree

I Want

I want to change myself for the better
But all I say to myself is that I'll do it later
It won't change the fact that yearning feeling to
get up and do something
That won't be just worth nothing

I mean, look at the people around me
They get up and get their plans set in stone
At least they don't get blown away by problems
That keeps them wondering if is it worth it in
bed with their pajama bottoms

I think to myself, instead of sitting and mopping,
I can keep growing and showing that little girl
That everything could be possible in this whirl
we call life
Despite what I want to do, I want to do it later

But there's so many things to do later
Makes my mind rush through endless
possibilities
That makes it feel like endless hostilities
What happens if I don't do it now?

What happens if I don't fulfill that promise?

What happens if I just sit there and let the world
keep going
While I am stuck not knowing
What I want to do

I want to be out there and here
Being with my friends and family
Trying to make time to open up
But never showing up

I want to stop that little voice from showing up
Telling me I am never going to be good enough
Leaving me to fend for myself in the rough
When looking for that lifesaver to show up

I want to show more than just that girl you get
those answers from
Because all she knows is that she knows where
she gets it from
When in reality I don't know what is going on
Around me and around you
Oh well, I may have to find out later
with all the other things I put on my silver
platter
All messy and full of things that depress me
But before I could figure out who, what, when,
where, and why

It's more that comes on the plate

That I want to figure out but now it has to be
later

Because now I want to be the best in school
Because I don't want to be on the cruel streets
But I already got to deal with defeats
Left and right

I already got to deal with people asking me
what's the right answer
Left and right
when I don't even know how you get the answer
I can't get to the destination without the
information
That I am getting from my education

Like how am I going to get into an Ivy League
With all the big ones in the leagues
Makes it seem like I am the weakest one
In the link

They say, "I have to stay ready, so you don't
have to get ready"
But how am I supposed to be ready for where I
am going to be
If I don't know if it's really where I want to be
Gosh, it's so many things I want to be

But I just can't do it right now.

Because now I gotta worry about how I want to
look
The world trying to judge me like a book
Look at her glasses, she's the nerd
Look at her body, those stretchmarks are
horrible
Look at her, look at how she acts

Look at the fact I am trying to live life
I am trying to live in time
Because time doesn't stop for no one
Like how I shouldn't be stopping for these
excuses
That keeps seducing the mind with its tempting
justifications

If I want to be something, I can work up from
nothing
And show them that I want to be something
But it ain't gotta be how you want it to be want

Let's talk about it

There are so many problems found in society
that no one talks
About. You probably thought one, whether one
of a
       MILLION coming in at once,
There is always a problem. However, there are
some that
can be solved with solutions. Whether...
Small or BIG,
Temporary or forever,
Stupid or smart,
We all try to solve something once every day.
Every day, there is something new that we wish
could go away.
              Wished we lived in a fairy tale
                      Where

happily ever after…

      Would stay forever…
But I hate to break it to you: this is the real
world.
In the real world, you have to face your problem.
In the real world, you think about how it affects
you.

In the real world, you have to think of the best
answer to solve it.

Those three steps seem easy, but you have to
make time to think about it.
Talk about it. I am sure you can do it, but do you
have the willpower to do it?
That question is not popular, but I would say
where it is asked:
The black community.

You have heard this before in different ways
Your momma got on you about those grades
When those names you keep hearing don't stay
out of the way
I can go on, and on, and on…

There are many ways of trying to do something.
Maybe for yourself, your best friend! The thing
is that YOU do it because YOU know it could
be beneficial or have a consequence. A
whooping, you ran to dodge it, we heard or
experienced that scary story before. The point is
that the consequences are not so…
FUN!
As we expect it to be. We try to change our
actions, but something stops us.
                Procrastination?

                        No!

Laziness?

Possibly, but no.
How about your mental health?
You might not believe me, but I will tell you a
little story about it.
There is a sixteen-year-old black girl named
Hope.
Always optimistic, very opportunistic
She was on her school's basketball team and
stayed on top

The girl would swift, swerve, and make goals
with no problem.
She got herself on some local magazine
columns,
But it was not as big as her championship game.

Hope had to stay in her lane and make sure there
were no excuses.
Either that, she loses or fuses. That kept
repeating, repeating--
until that unfortunate call. That call would
forever change her game.
Cut to the case: Her mother fainted and was now
in the hospital.

We expect Hope to tell her coach that she needs
to go home, but she has to keep her throne.
Make her mother proud, right?

She decides to take deep breaths and get on that
court.
With her mother as support, she fought to do her
best.
Her mother keeps popping up in her head.
          Is she okay?
                              What happened?
                                        She
might be going through something…
          IS SHE GOING TO GET WORSE?

IS SHE GOING TO… DIE?!

Hope can not believe this. She sits there and her
mind
goes wild.
Her breathing gets faster, her hands get clammy,
So much going on and on about her important
family
Leaving her unhappy, and confused, like a
possible failure.

You might think she is extra, but we have so
much on our plates.
Work, family, school, our relationships.

We can not balance it all the time.
One thing is that the plate is empty, and then life
fills it back up.
We are expected to sort it out, but it is not
always easy.

That is where mental health matters.
It could startle you and make you scatter, but it
is here to stay.
It affects how you think, feel, and act.
How could Hope handle her stress without
feeling attacked?

I say take deep breaths.
                              In and out,
                                        In and
out,

            In and out
What do you think happened to Hope?
Did she...
A) Go crazy on her coach
B) Do a cartwheel because it'll drag attention
C) Soothe her
D) Make her hungry. I am hungry for a toaster
strudel.

D sounds right, but C is correct.

Hope sees that maybe it is not her time on the
court
but rather the time to support her mother.
She tells her coach that she needs to play another
time,
Might lose your prime, she says.

Hope knows that at that moment, she can
prioritize herself.
She can prioritize her mother and her health.
She can prioritize her mental health.
You can believe that mental health is too much
itself,
but you never realize that these tasks you do for
yourself all work under
This.

In this world, you can be weak. Strong.
Powerful. Afraid.
It all depends on what YOU do for YOU.
So do not forget that your mental health is there,
but do you have the willpower to care?

A Soul's Fragile Care

How can I love you,
If you never wanted me there for you?
You used to be the one that made me feel at
home,
Able to get away from all this stress and the
unknown
Knowing that there was always someone to hold
me
In their arms because they wanted to assure me
Everything will be okay as long as you have me

But, where were you when I needed you?
When life threw hard jabs at me,
losing my dad, having to help my mom alone
leaving me there to plea that everything will get
better,
Hoping that you would be there to keep me
altogether
You know where I found you?

I found you having to choose between being a
boy or a man
Who told me that he would never hurt me
because he had a plan

To be the one who cherished me and made me
feel special
But it seems you failed to stick to your plan
Rather be the one to hurt someone you love than
be a man

I did not love you to hurt you,
But it was because I saw greatness within you
I wanted to see you through, inside and out
Past that little nerdy smile and those dreads
Making me go all red whenever you
remembered
all the little things to the end

You knew my favorite artist, so you got an
album for me
You knew that I loved plushies, so you won
them all for me
You knew that I love mementos, so you made
them with me
You knew everything, yet you treated me like
nothing
So how am I to push past through all this
knowing
That you never thought of my love for such
things

I yearned to be around you every second of the
day,

You were the first person I woke to say,
"Good morning! How did you sleep well?"
Knowing that deep down there was someone
past that harsh shell
And could tell me everything for as long as time
could tell

You were the one out of everyone that I would
push through crowds for,
The one that I would run through the hallways
for,
The one that I would fight any girl for,
The one that I would end up walking down the
aisle for,
The one that I would never lose my hope for,
and somehow I wish I had taken all of this back
before

Before this, I told you three things
before we started this new chapter of our lives
Respect me and I respect you,
Care for me and I care for you,
Give me hope and the same goes for you,
Notice how I did everything for you

Yet you never wanted me there for you?
--
You were everything, you make it seem like I
never did anything

when all I did was put everything aside for all
the things
That I could ever do for you, spending years
Knowing that I am the only man who will burst
my back
For you because no other woman was made like
You

I know you are hurt, I know that you are scared
Are you thinking that I am going to leave you
out there
For the next boy to play your heart and leave it
there
No! That was never my intention, I always try to
approach prevention
Knowing that all I am focused on is getting your
attention
To let you know that I am the one trying to love
you

Into someone who is a lost soul,
Trying to find someone to fill that empty hole
That made you feel whole and gave you control
Of the one thing you could lose
No, I am not making excuses, and not here
To force you to choose what is right

I know that cheating on you was not right
I know that when those tears fell down your face

You would see me as a joke, as a disgrace
I mean, you already put me in my place
But all I care about is fixing my mistakes
So you can take me back with some grace

I loved you ever since freshman year of high
school,
I fell so hard that day and my friends called me a
fool.
They wanted to follow the rule that only touch
first base
That is the only place they know
But I know I want you so
Because I knew we could grow
We grow up and graduate together,
Me and you going to Howard together,
We might be in different classes however
Better when we meet at the center
And find pleasure altogether
Because we can have it whenever

You have to believe me,
Although we are just seventeen,
True love is not seen often
So maybe do not take this pain to your coffin
Because I rather feel awful
Than seeing you being ripped out of my life

Senior year might be too much

And I sound corny when saying this
I miss your touch and when we had lunch
No one to rush our time together
Which made my day
Having you will make my day until the end of
time
--
You and me had such a chance
but you tore it up right in my face
You cannot reverse your mistakes
There is no escape
From feeling constant regret

You should have thought this all out
Looked into that girl's eyes
And knew that this was not mine
You are built with lies
You are so unwise

If you had time to care,
We would not even be there
To the point where this will not work
This affair worked to destroy us
And it all makes sense

How can I love you,
If you never wanted me there for you?

they say a black girl like me

should straighten my hair
because my hair goes everywhere
free and bare for the world to see
but if it is curly or kinky to a degree
then they all agree that my hair shall be tamed

I try to relax my hair, but how can I relax it
when it takes enough hair wraps to keep it
together
enough oils to keep it moisturized
enough appointments to keep it right
because a girl like me has to sit for hours
making sure she looks right

those braids and locs that protect us
from the harsh expectations
that we have held for generations and
generations
that say we are not beautiful but rather
monsters in our armor

They say our hair is too messy,
Too nappy, too unmanageable,
Too feral, but it has been said more than once
that my hair is not a part of me to fuss about

But to be proud of, no doubt about that

a girl like me with her hair done
should look better than she was yesterday
because there will be better days
when no one has to tell her who she should be
today

Come! Look into her wardrobe
so much style all while that confidence grows
but you say she shows too much
those crop tops seem to attract the wrong eye
with short skirts that lead the lustful eye

It is too tight! Too short! It is just not right,
how can a black girl wear this with this body?
maybe if she covered her body with these baggy
clothes,
but now new accusations arose
It is too boyish! It does not suit you,

Are you trying to be like those gangsters on the
street?

black girls from afar have heard it in many
forms,
from their mammas to their sisters to their
friends

it all depends, but how long will those judging
let it extend?
you cannot follow this trend and judge black
girls
I highly recommend piping down on your words

let us not jump on the boat wagon that
ALL black girls dress with no control
but don't get it twisted
we had it under control for generations,
so do not tell us about no expectations

You say a black girl should look like this
there are things we should not miss
or try to change
but how are you going to change a girl's beauty
trying to make it your eternal duty?

You say a black girl should have hips and thighs
so that they can talk about their prize but
do you see more than that?
despite all she brings to the table,
you are still unable to see her true beauty

You say a black girl should have full lips
Not too small, not too large
but just right to let your lips do the talking
and not hear the girl talking and trying to
understand you

while you are trying to lay hands to play with
her
for she is

You say a black girl should be this, should be
that
but lemme me tell you a fact
these black girls can live through them and make
an impact
we attract excellence, we attract the message
that
a black girl like me
can be whoever can be whoever she wants to be

You, wired into tomorrow

Remember when your mother always brings up
That back in her day, she used to be outside
consuming sunlight
And was not expecting for us to be looking into
blue lights
that controls society day and night
No idea that how it might shape generations

For years, we always seem to judge what our
phones are
Older generations say it is a distraction, never
able to understand our actions
Our parents say that it could either make or
break us
Our friends connect on there to find us or to
relax from life
Sometimes, life never gives us time

We need time to focus on our grind,
We need time to find out wassup,
See if we caught up or not up with our work,
With so many things on our minds, we need a
place to put some things aside,
but do you know how much a phone provides?

Our phones are where we find out everything
When carrying the internet and many other things,
From being able to find jobs to exploring ways
of how to not be so bored out of your mind,
How would you not want to use it for everything?

Everything is constantly moving, never stopping
Even when watching something, you do not think
That the amount of videos you scrolled on
Took your time in a blink with the amount of a
click, click, click?

But what about the others who use it to think?
Who use it to create something great?
There is no place for debate, things are set straight
That a phone is not only an update
But an update for you to see

The future generation.

"In 24 Hours"

My mother shall hand the world to me,
as it is now in my domain, allowing me to see
Beyond the colored glasses that I once worse,
now shattered
trying to put the pieces back together, but she
pats my back
telling me as long as I stay proud of being black
There shall be no harm holding me back

She told me she had explored this world with me
for too long,
been there to hold me strong along through the
huge waves,
Suddenly, we are hit and our arms are unlinked
I try to reach for her, but they have restricted
me--
the darkness consuming me, my fear controlling
me
For I wake up in a world where no one looks
like me

All these smiley faces, trying to familiarize me
with this place
The high waves have taken control, the pace
seems to be going further

and further away from my grasp, how shall I
tread lightly
if this sudden shift has changed course so
slightly
Enough for me to fall deeper and deeper into the
darkness
No one to keep me further away from this strong
drift

The moment I can gain at least some solace
comes from a stranger who has found
themselves with a promise
to be able to tread the waters freely within
unlimited security
for they came to this unfamiliar place with a
guide
and someone who understands them in the long
ride
Oh, how I wish I could do that

College does not even sound real
How can I even grasp this feeling
of loneliness, of despair, of disconnection
but I do not see anyone that is a reflection of me
So how can I find a connection besides the
person I am trying to build
within me

The waters seem too hostile, enough to leave me
fragile
I sit here, eyes straight ahead, how long shall
this dread stay?
I feel myself drifting away until she takes me out
She notices that I have gained doubt throughout
this route
as the captain of this boat, as the captain of my
life
Why have I lost myself staying afloat?

The world, the domain, the game, the heavy
waters
Whatever life seems to go by, there are so many
things I cannot deny
Controlling this ship is too much,
trying to control my life
feels more of a rush these days
Maybe this could be a never ending phase

She assures me that while the waters weigh me
down,
there is still a way to set myself and stay around
allowing myself to stay bound for what I am
here for
To inspire, to create, to prosper
For if no one could stop her, what makes me
think
they shall stop me?

For the waves are only the rocky parts,
They are not every part of this experience
While I steer inexperienced, knowing what I
want is serious
I keep myself cautious and knowing
The dream of having an education as an
African-American
Is surely enough to hold as the American dream
as I journey through this endless sea we call
'life'.

"04.24.24"

Deandre
Loving son and brother
Died at the young age of sixteen
Surrounded by loved ones and a sobbing mother
who lost one of her sons,
He will be remembered by his family,
but not remembered as another victim at the
hands of a gun

A bullet was found in his heart, his right arm,
and his shoulder
Had time to rush him to the hospital, hoping to
see that one-line move
Only to be removed from the bed and into a
gurney
Covered by a white sheet, the cycle on repeat
His family left wondering what to do on these
streets

They leave flowers, candles, balloons--
A way to connect to the dead, a silent way to
spread the message
That Deandre was a young man heading towards
a good path

Already given scholarships for college,
acknowledged as top of the class
Ready to walk the stage, but only
He is on stage and now they all have to look
down on him slowly

"What has my boy ever done to deserve this?"
He was going places, he needed to walk a few
stages
So he could learn to create the change that could
never change
If only someone stepped up--
If only someone like Deandre lived longer to
create the change

His funeral was hosted at 12: 45 p.m..,
Here lies a boy full of ambition, paid to go to
college on full tuition
In no such position to even grasp the possibility
of being given an opportunity
in a community where they believe we shall fail,
shall crumble,
Only live to thrive in such troubling times with
these crimes
Because some believe the boy was the reason for
this crime

Before his death, at 7:15 a.m.

Kiana, a little girl who loved to play with her
dolls
Held it tight in her tiny arms
Looking into the sky as if pleading, hoping
That someone would come to save her from
choking
On her blood

Police called it a shame, a terrible thing
Too many photos to take and bring
To the stations, but ONE bullet came
Hit her right in the poor lung,
Her weeps of pain were the last thing she sung

A mother, who once dressed her
Who once held and told her I loved her
Is now wondering if there will be justice for her
If a little girl like her could die,
Then what about the other little girls who looked
like her?

Who dreamed like her? Who loved dolls like
her?
No one will be able to be like her daughter,
No one will be able to sing her heart like her,
Her mother now in tears
As her friends watch and surround her
Wondering if it were a chance to ever gain those
years back

On her grave, it now reads:
Kiana Kay
Born August 15, 2018, died April 14, 2024
Loving daughter and granddaughter
She is outlived by her mother,
Kiana was an only child that cared about
wanting to change for others

Hours later, after both funerals,
Police got a report at 4:34 pm that two best
friends walking home from school
Was caught in a crossfire, Tiana laid out on the
ground
The other holding her as his tears fell and looked
around
Screaming and screaming, hoping that they
would make it

When they made it, Tiana was already gone
Her friend, Booker, was left beyond words
Was in full denial and only when he walked
down that aisle
He realized this was not a joke,
Hoped for so long until he fell and broke down
Shutting down himself

Minutes later, Booker mustered up the courage
To go up those stairs and near the speaker

Maybe speak about how he feels,
What he will not forget, but
He decides to speak about the community

Ladies and gentlemen, I am sure you have
noticed
If I was not there, my friend would have been
road dust
I wanted to be there for her in that moment,
because there are moments like this
Where people miss the opportunity to take these
hits
And do not call quits

I have worked and worked to keep her alive,
Realizing that we need to make sure this
community survive
From the bullets that have ripped through our
lives
Making us lose the people we loved in our lives
Losing years and no change, we need to realize
things
Need to change or our fears will grow

Grow into something more dangerous than
losing lives,
but fearing that we would lose lives walking
home,
Making us think if this is our home

Some of us grew immune and let this go,
Realizing this will be our lives for as long as it goes
But what if there is more than we know?

We know that this is the #1 reason the black community suffers,
Because we lose our sisters and brothers
Not easy to recover, but we can know from one another
We can stop the cycle of letting another mother
Suffer these repercussions, knowing we got the instructions
To create change

Nothing is unchanging except change itself,
The only thing that stays constant is change itself,
I know it will be hard for me, but I know I am not the only one thinking this to myself
I need to help, I am not letting no one else
Turn out next on the scene, next on the news
And next in a grave

We are called a community,
We are in unity under the same struggle,
I know there was not one time we believed the trouble
Would find their way into our homes

because of how far a bullet can go
that we had to move further away from the
window than we can go

If we can realize that April 14th and the day
before that,
We have lost more than one, two, or three lives,
We have lost more lives than that,
But let us not be so taken back by the past,
So we can focus on our next act,
So we can create an impact

"History's breath into our lives"

We breathe, we see, we believe
that we can achieve what we are meant to be
We are the future of our nation, full of education
Ready for any situation, no worries about our
location
Because our education is our inspiration,
Our information that we can keep for
the population

The population sees this as a race,
already seeing us as a disgrace due to our race,
but they do not know our case and
cannot erase how we got to this place,
as we embrace who allowed us to create
So we do not have to stay in place

As our history is our identity,
So why try to turn it against us
And make it our enemy?

"Well, it seems"

51

Teens' dreams
do not have breaks.

"Breaking the shell"

I have no idea where I should go
       But what I do know is that I am trapped
in this shell,
I could crack it so easily,
       But the layers have recently left me
drowsy.
There is no opening, so focusing on the voices
has been no choice
       I try to avoid angering them so they
shall not destroy
me more than I already am.
       Why is she so quiet, so naive? I want to
achieve
so much, but I have to believe.
       I have to believe that what I perceive
       Is not make-believe.
I have a goal within my control,
I know how much it has for a role,
But I feel myself falling deeper
           And

Deeper

                  Into
        This
     Hole

Where
     I
wonder if this is farewell to my last chance
And let myself give up as a whole?
Would you believe me if I told you that I got the
shell once?
             When I was younger and free, we could
all agree
This shell has never grown until a degree
when suddenly kids who could count to one,
two, three,
were now pushing me to a certain degree
   As I sat under the tree and wondered what
shall be the key
I would never expect this shell to grow
                     Upon me.
The things I once used to love,
                             now shoved to

the side,
Has left me wondering
Who can I love
What can I love
When can I love
Where can I love
Why can I love

If the shell makes it easier for me to give myself
away,
             Because trying to stay keeps me at bay,

As the days grow by suddenly
Maybe it is okay to stay in this shell for today

But what about tomorrow?
            What about a few days later when this
shell,
My protector, my director, my inspector
Has left this terrible effect where I feel like
nothing
And even if I do something
            Could it be the one thing that prevents
sme from becoming
The one thing I find myself running
                                    from?

I want to be something,
            But the shell makes me
feel
Like nothing,   but suddenly
When I find myself   with them,
The people who love me,   the things that
shape me,
Create me,   Like this shell
has tried to do to me,
            I realize the only thing
            Breaking was this shell and
                  Now it is time I say
farewell

And

leave this cell.

"perfection is not always the direction"

You ever wondered about the worst day in history?
Opening up my AP results was since it could take my glory
Understanding that only the most successful could put it on their Instagram story
Answers and answers, I need them! Everyone is
Ready across the globe including me, the girl wishing
Every score across the board is higher than a four. Time to get
Going and reading these results, ready to open in three, two, one..!
Oh my god, I got a four!
Oh my god, I got a..one?!
Do not play jokes because I am not the one to joke!
Easy to say it could be just a mistake.
Nothing like a little reset could put me in place.
Oh boy, maybe I am not good enough
Underestimating that maybe I am not good like the rest
Going to have to admit that I am not fit for this test

However, I remembered I learned one thing
from the best,
Never let yourself be put down, especially from
a test.
Oh, yeah. I just caught that maybe I am just
being too hard on myself
Maybe the real test was to see how much faith I
had in myself
And although it sounds corny, I can not put this
on the shelf
Trying too hard to uphold being the smart one
but never
Trying to release the pressure of trying to be
perfect
Effort was enough, so that was enough
Realizing that I scored higher on one makes me
feel glad
What I needed to realize was that being said
would never bring me to the truth
Having pride is what I'll choose on this smooth
ride so
As I sat there and closed the computer, I realized
That I am good enough, no matter what

"A breakthrough"

People do not like to listen
They rather look around and glisten
at the fact they are deaf, blind, unaware
of the inevitable truth that
We are here

We have been here for so long,
sat on the sidelines planning, thinking, creating
The ever-growing possibilities of building
an opportunity that shows our
Abilities

You might wonder…what are our abilities?
One could dance their heart out,
sing their heart out,
fight their heart out,
Hell, you can write your heart out

I do not write to show that I can do it,
I write for the people who need it
No one is getting left on this list
especially teens who know they can commit
because I know there is nothing called
'Quits'

We heard this fifty times, we cannot admit
that we said this fifty times or more
because sometimes we need time
To say that we are fine

I mean, we are human after all,
We are either in confusion or left in ruins
But we always want to find ourselves in a
resolution
because that leads to the best conclusion
It has been proven

One way or another, you will find a way to
thrive
because we all have our lives
We know what we need to survive
You are your guide
You need to provide
On this long ride

Speaking of long rides, we are near the end
The children who once used to spend their time
outside
thrown inside for one graduation
just to get thrown back into college applications
I wonder how on Earth we got to this
conversation
Of whether or not I am hallucinating

It is rather crazy we are thrown into the real
world
We heard these words and possibly heard
this from a specific history teacher
Either way, if you know how to count and stay
en route
then it does not matter if you are cute cause
You gonna have to stay ready

I will tell you, from writer to writer,
Teen to teen, human to human
that every story needs three things
Conflict, character, change
We are at the turning page
And at the final age of our lives

We can make our own decisions
with our visions
I remember those five years ago
where I never knew my
voice would make noise,
I would not avoid
what I enjoyed

As a senior now, I look
back and then at this story
and I tell you this in glory
that if a Black girl like me
Could make all these stories

For teens, for her community, for herself,
Then do the best for yourself

"Free yourself"

because you never know if
you are the one holding yourself back.

www.ingramcontent.com/pod-product-compliance
Lightning Source LLC
LaVergne TN
LVHW051229200726
843510LV00011B/1524